London-born Arnold Schwartzman is a renowned graphic designer and the recipient of the Academy Award® as producer and director of the feature documentary "Genocide" (1981), and author of a number of books on the subject of 18th, 19th and 20th century architecture.

In 1982 he was appointed the Director of Design for the 1984 Los Angeles Olympic Games.

Among his recent design projects are two murals for Cunard's MS Queen Elizabeth, and the U.N. Peace Bell Monument, Seoul, South Korea.

In 2002, Schwartzman was appointed an Officer of the Order of the British Empire (OBE), and in 2006 was conferred the distinction of Royal Designer (RDI) by the Royal Society of Arts.

Arnold lives in Los Angeles, and works in collaboration with his wife, Isolde.

Cover:
Fresco,
La Samaritaine
department store,
1905–10.
Rue de Rivoli and
Quai du Louvre,
Paris, France.
Architect:
Henri Sauvage.
Artist:
Francis Jourdain,
1876–1958.

Endpapers:
Wallpaper,
Hotel Tassel, 1892–1893.
Rue Paul-Emile Janson 6,
Brussels, Belgium.
Architect:
Victor Horta,
1861–1947.

ART NOUVEAU

METROPOLITAIN

The World's Most Beautiful Buildings
from Guimard to Gaudi

ART NOUVEAU

Arnold Schwartzman

PALAZZO

Right:
Isolde, 1895,
Illustration, The Studio.
Artist:
Aubrey Beardsley.

Half Title:
Decorative tiles,
Michelin House, 1911,
Michelin Tyre
Company Ltd.,
81 Fulham Road,
Chelsea, London, UK.
Pictorial panels design:
Gilardoni Fils, Paris.

Frontis piece:
Cast iron and glass,
Paris Metro station, 1900,
Porte Dauphine,
(Jean de Lattre de Tassigny),
Paris, France.
Architect:
Hector Guimard.
Architect:
Hector Guimard,
1867–1942.

Title page:
Detail,
brass mail slot,
Smidswater 26,
The Hague,
The Netherlands.
Architect:
Johannes Petrus
Josephus Lorrie,
1861–1944.

Contents page:
Decorative cartouche,
Paris Metro station, 1900,
Porte Dauphine,
(Jean de Lattre de Tassigny),
Paris, France.
Architect:
Hector Guimard.

Dedication

To my wife and
creative partner Isolde
who has lovingly
infused her magic potion
into this book.

Acknowledgments

Paul Boudens
Gert Dumbar
Steve Heller
Robert Nichols
Marie Parache
Mireille Swinnen
Alice Twemlow
Michael Webb

First published in 2023 by Palazzo Editions Ltd
15 Church Road
London, SW 3 9HE
www.palazzoeditions.com

Text © 2023 Arnold Schwartzman
Design and layout copyright © 2023 Arnold Schwartzman

All rights reserved. No part of this publication may be reproduced in any form or by any means — electronic, mechanical, photocopying, recording, or otherwise — or stored in any retrieval system of any nature without prior written permission from the copyright holders.
Arnold Schwartzman has asserted his moral right to be identified as the author of this work in accordance with the Copyright, Designs and Patents Act of 1988.
Every effort has been made to trace and acknowledge the copyright holders.
If any unintentional omission has occurred, we would be pleased to add an appropriate acknowledgment in any future edition of the book.
A CIP catalogue record for this book is available from the British Library.
Hardback ISBN 9781786750631

Bound and printed in China
10 9 8 7 6 5 4 3 2 1

Contents

Introduction

From Guimard to Gaudi

Right:
Mosaic,
The Five Continents,
Société Générale,
Rue de Sèvres 6,
Paris, France.

Opposite:
Façade,
Lavirotte Building,
1901,
Avenue Rapp 29,
Paris, France.
Architect:
Jules Aimé Lavirotte,
1864–1924.

Do you recall the first time you saw the film "Gigi"? Set in Paris during the period known as La Belle Epoch, Gigi, a schoolgirl, pays a visit to her aunt whose home turns out to be the iconic Jules Lavirotte-designed mansion at 29 Avenue Rapp.

A recent viewing of the film brought back so many fond memories of my childhood days when I spent my school holidays visiting my great aunt in Paris. My postcards sent home described the many memorable sites I was taken to, including the Eiffel Tower, erected as part of the Paris 1900 Exposition. From the premiere étage I surveyed the panoramic vista of the Ville des Lumières. Stamps in my 1947 passport bear witness to my visits to Printemps and Galleries Lafayette, two of the city's "grands magasins", where I exchanged my sterling into francs. My aunt drew my attention to the stores' magnificent stained glass ceilings, informing me that they were glorious remnants from the Art Nouveau period.

At that time I was not aware of the subtleties of the distinct styles of architecture. It was much later that I learnt that the term Art Nouveau was taken from the name of Siegfried Bing's 1895 Paris emporium of that name. The Art Nouveau movement was an offspring of the British Arts & Crafts movement. Among its major protagonists were Arthur Heygate Mackmurdo, William Morris and Charles Rennie Mackintosh, who had collectively decided to turn their backs on the mass production of the century's Industrial Revolution and to produce handcrafted wares. These latterday medievalists sought a return to the Middle Ages of Camelot, accompanied by their Pre Raphaelite compatriots, which included Dante Gabriel Rossetti and Edward Burne-Jones. Their field of creativity embraced textiles, wall-paper, furniture, books, household products, and last but not least, architecture.

29

Other British precursors of the movement include illustrators Aubrey Beardsley, Walter Crane and the Beggerstaff Brothers. The new movement navigated its way from the Clyde to the Thames, onto the Seine and the Rhine, through to the Danube, the Bosphorous, the Volga, Swartrivier, Kanda River and to the banks of the Hudson. Indeed, the movement permeated throughout the Five Continents. As early as the 1880s, Art Nouveau spread to embrace the Lowlands, where Belgian architects such as Victor Horta and Henry van de Velde excelled.

In France, the country's two centers of creativity were Paris and Nancy. In Paris, on Avenue Rapp, Jules Lavirotte entertained us with his sexually provocative brand of architecture. Hector Guimard dazzled the city's commuters with his Style Metro underground station entrances and ornate signage, which was in stark contrast to the more conservative letterforms of Edward Johnston's San Serif font for the London Underground.

Toulouse-Lautrec frequently found his inspiration in the woodcut prints of the Japanese masters Hiroshige and Hokusai which were sometimes found lining imported tea chests. This influence from the Orient can be seen in the paintings of Gauguin, Munch, Steinlen, Bonnard and Klimt, plus the American James McNeill Whistler (he chronicled on canvas my birthplace of Wapping, London). His painting, "La princesse du pays de la porcelaine", now housed in the Freer Gallery of Art, Washington, DC, once graced the London dining room of the home of his patron Frederick Leyland.

Other American artists include Maxfield Parrish, and Louis Tiffany, who flourished with his opalescent stained glass creations. In the mid-20th century his lamps fell out of fashion, however today they are much sought-after.

"Der Zeit ihre Kunst". (To every age its art.)

As the movement spread, Vienna had its Hoffman, Loos, Wagner, and Moser and his graphic out-pourings of the Wiener Werkstätte, and Prague gave us Mucha's lithographic posters. These exponents of the movement displayed their unique individual skills for us to witness and enjoy to this day.

Above:
Wiener Werkstätte logo, 1903.
Designer:
Koloman Moser, 1868–1918.

The French term "Art Nouveau" took on other names. In Austria it was known as Wiener Jugendstil after the artists of the Vienna Secession. In neighboring countries a similar style emerged, namely Secessionsstil in Germany and in the Netherlands Niewe Kunst, in Hungary Szecesszió, Secese in Czechoslovakia and in Italy, Stile Liberty.

In Barcelona one discovers Modernist Antoni Gaudi's more flamboyant expression of the style. In contrast to the black-spewing pea-souper chimneys of the London fog of my youth, I discovered a frozen arabesque of dancing chimney pots at Gaudí's Casa Batlló.

Marble and mosaic decoration, Zum weissen Engel (White Angel) pharmacy, 1901–02, Bognerstrasse 9, Vienna, Austria. Artist: Oskar Laske, 1871–1951.

Traveling on to the cusp of Asia to Istanbul, Turkey, I was surprised to find, among the city's Byzantine mosques, Art Nouveau architecture very much akin to that of Paris, while in Slovenia, Jože Plecnik delighted us with his own unique brand of the style.

On a visit to Japan, I discovered an Art Nouveau structure, the former 1921 Hiroshima Prefectorial Products Exhibition building designed by the Czech architect Jan Letzel, its remants today, post the atom bomb, are the Gerbaku Dome Hiroshima Peace Memorial.

A muster of peacocks, a parliament of owls and a swarm of dragonflies – the observer can find examples of these winged creatures graphically nested in virtually every country where Art Nouveau blossomed, interpreted in a variety of artistic forms. The movement's decoration was also inspired by organic plant forms. In Antwerp and Brussels I came across façades blooming with lilies, sunflowers, daffodils and bluebells, beautifully rendered on mosaic, tile and sgraffito.

In my adopted home of Hollywood, California, I could not find any evidence of the Art Nouveau style, save that of the film industry's Oscar®-winning art production for "Gigi", "My Fair Lady", and "Moulin Rouge", bringing awareness of the style to the cinema-going public.

London's tiled Michelin House brought a touch of Paris to the somewhat somber city. Hotel Solvay's door number, 224 Avenue Louise, Brussels, reminded me of the daunting task of selecting the very best of my photographs for the 224 pages of this book.

In conclusion, allow me the opportunity to take you on a virtual stroll along the boulevards, Strassen, straats, stradas, calles and ulicas, to share this treasure trove of some of the world's finest Art Nouveau architecture.

Hollywood, California, 2023

Above:
Gilded bronze bust,
Gustave Eiffel, 1929,
Eiffel Tower,
Paris, France.
Sculptor:
Antoine Bourdelle,
1861–1929.

France

Right:
Cast iron and glass
Metro entrance,
Porte Dauphine
(Jean de Lattre
de Tassigny) Station,
1900.
Paris, France.
Architect:
Hector Guimard.

Right:
Metro station sign, 1900s,
Paris, France.
Architect:
Hector Guimard.

Below:
Decorative panels,
Metro entrance,
Porte Dauphine
(Jean de Lattre
de Tassigny) Station, 1900,
Paris, France.
Architect:
Hector Guimard.

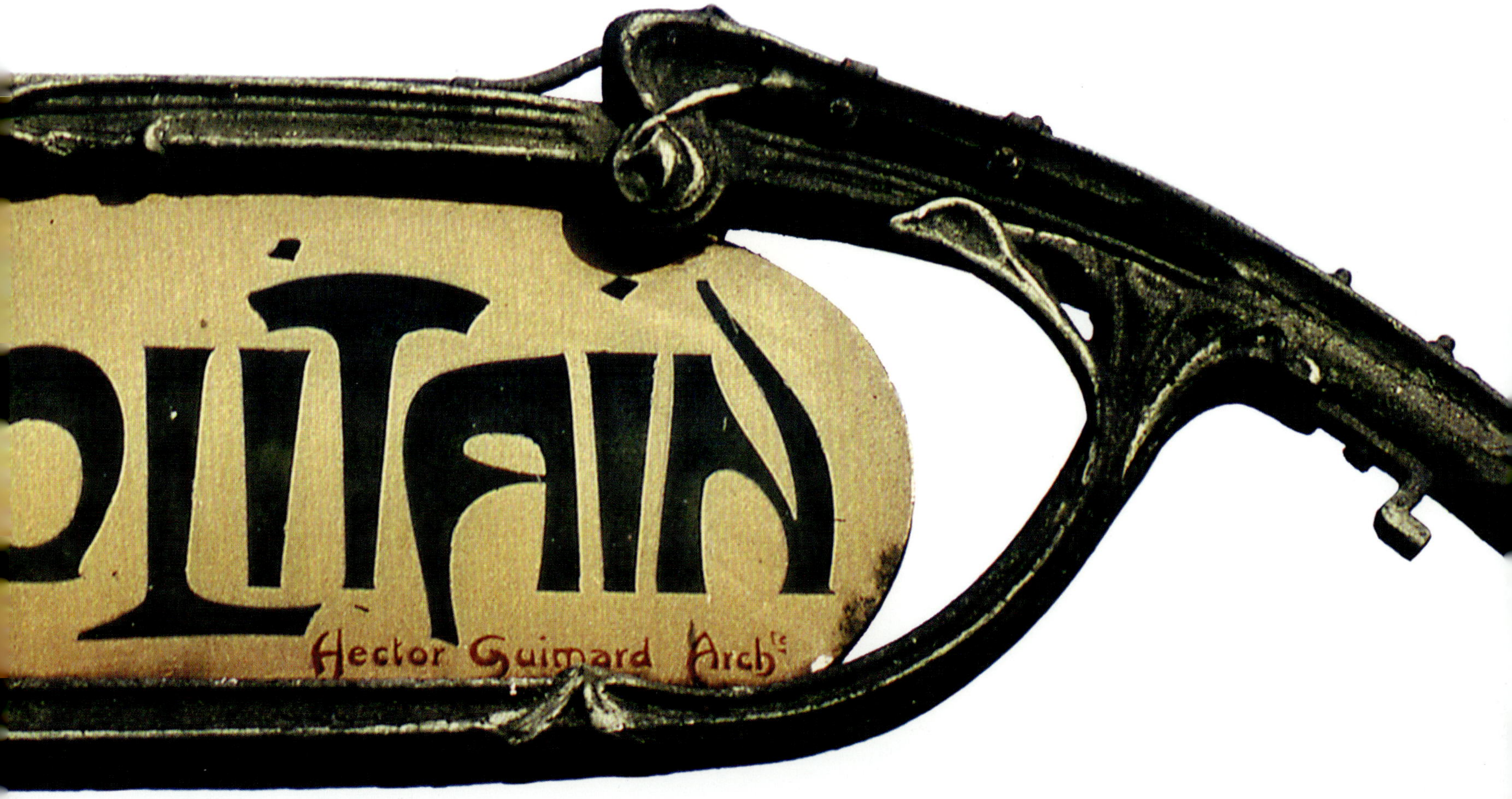
Hector Guimard Archte

Above:
French postage stamp.

Right:
Green wrought iron,
Metro station entrance,
Abbesses Station, 1912,
Montmartre,
Paris, France.
Architect:
Hector Guimard.

Famille Ernest Caillat
Sepulchre, 1899,
Pere Lachaise Cemetery,
8 Boulevard de Menilmnant,
Paris, France.
Design: Hector Guimard.

Above:
House number 14,
this page:
Balcony, cast iron masks,
and opposite:
entrance gate,
glazed sandstone façade,
apartment building,
Le Castel Béranger,
1894–98.
Rue Jean de la Fontaine 14,
Paris, France.
Architect:
Hector Guimard.

IMMEUBLE PRIMÉ
AU 1ER CONCOURS DE FAÇADES
DE LA VILLE DE PARIS
Hector GUIMARD Architecte 1897-98
14
CASTEL BERANGER

This page and opposite:
Details,
Lavirotte Building, 1901,
Avenue Rapp 29,
Paris, France.
Architect:
Jules Aimé Lavirotte.

Note:
See façade page 7.

Above:
Door handle,
Maxims, 1893,
Rue Royale 7,
Paris, France.

Right and below:
Lizard door handles,
1899,
Rue de Grenelle 151,
Paris, France.
Architect:
Jules Aimé Lavirotte.

Opposite:
Entrance door, 1899,
Rue de Grenelle 151,
Paris, France.
Architect:
Jules Aimé Lavirotte.

Above:
Fountain,
right and opposite:
Front doors,
home of
Jules Aimé Lavirotte,
1899–1900,
Square Rapp 3,
Paris, France.
Architect:
Jules Aimé Lavirotte.

Right:
Façade, 1910–13,
and below:
Tile detail,
Former home of the architect, now an apartment building, Rue Belliard 185, Paris, France.
Architect:
Henri Deneux, 1874–1969.

Opposite:
Tile illustration of architect Henri Deneux at work, 1910–13, Rue Belliard 185, Paris, France.
Architect:
Henri Deneux.

Abel, shop sign, 1845,
Passage Jouffroy 36,
10–12 Blvd Montmartre,
Paris, France.
Architects:
François-Hippolyte
Distailleur and
Romaine de Bourges.

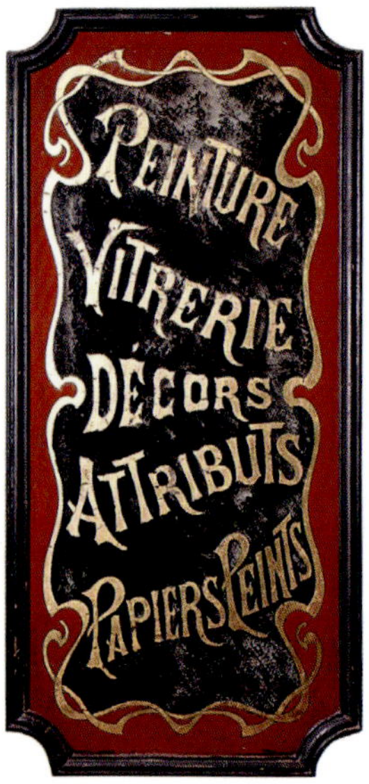

Above:
French gilded
trade shop sign, 1900s.

Right:
Horsemeat
butcher shop, 1900s,
Rue Le Pic 30,
Montmartre,
Paris, France.

36

30

Above:
Detail,
right and opposite:
Tiles,
Le Petit Zinc restaurant,
1900,
Rue Saint Benoit 11,
Paris, France.

Right and opposite:
Façade,
artist studios, 1911,
Rue Campagne-Première 31,
Paris, France.
Architect:
Andre Arfidson.
Ceramist:
Alexandre Bigot,
1862–1969.

Right:
Entrance door
flanked by door plates,
artist studios, 1911,
Rue Campagne-Première 31,
Paris, France.
Architect:
Andre Arfidson.
Ceramist:
Alexandre Bigot.

This page and opposite:
Boutique Fouquet, jewellery store interior details, 1901, Musée Carnavalet, Rue Royale George 6, Paris, France. Designer: Alphonse Mucha, 1860–1939.

Boutique Fouquet, jewellery store front and interior details, 1901, Musée Carnavalet, Rue Royale George 6, Paris, France. Designer: Alphonse Mucha.

Above: Alphonse Mucha's signature.

QUET

Mosaic signage,
La Samaritaine
department store,
1905–10,
9 Rue de la Monnaie,
Paris, France.
Architect:
Frantz Jourdain,
1847–1935.
Mosaic:
Henri Bichi,
1855–n/a.

Mosaic signage,
La Samaritaine
department store,
1905–10,
Rue de Rivoli and
Quai du Louvre,
Paris, France.
Architects:
Frantz Jourdain
and Henri Sauvage.

ITAINE

RITAINE
CHASSE

Above:
Mosaic floor,
and right:
Upper floor
peacock fresco,
La Samaritaine
department store,
1905–10,
Rue de Rivoli and
Quai du Louvre,
Paris, France.
Artist:
Francis Jourdain,
1876–1958.

Façade,
Au Printemps
department Store, 1911,
Boulevard Haussmann 64,
Paris, France.
Architect:
René Binet.

Opposite:
Detail,
tinted glass cupola,
Tea Room,
Au Printemps
department Store, 1911,
Boulevard Haussmann 64,
Paris, France.
Architect:
René Binet,
1866–1911.
Glass design:
Eugène Briere,
1858–1932.

Above:
Metal plaque,
Paris, France.
Architect:
Hector Guimard.

Right:
Balcony,
Avenue Mozart 122,
Paris, France.
Architect:
Hector Guimard.

Right:
Iron balcony,
Trémois Building, 1909,
Rue François-Millet,
Paris, France.
Architect:
Hector Guimard.

Above:
Street name sign, 1900s,
Rue Agar,
Paris, France.

Left:
Cast iron balcony railing,
1909–11,
Rue La Fontaine 19
and Rue Agar,
Paris, France.
Architect:
Hector Guimard.

Right and below:
Façade and detail,
The House of Lilies, 1900,
Rue du Champ de Mars 33,
Paris, France.
Architect:
Octave Raquin,
1826–1913.

Right:
House number,
Hotel Mezzara, 1910–11,
Rue de la Fontaine 60,
Paris, France.
Architect:
Hector Guimard.

Opposite:
Façade,
Ceramic Hotel, 1904–34,
Avenue Wagram,
Paris, France.
Architect:
Jules Aimé Lavirotte.
Ceramicist:
Alexandre Bigot,
1862–1927.

GRÈS
BIGOT

Front door,
Rue Victor Schoelcher 5,
1911,
Paris, France.
Architect:
Paul Follot,
1877–1941.
Ceramist:
Alexandre Bigot.

Above:
Door handles.
Paris, France.

Right:
Front door, 1903–04.
Rue de Trétaigne 7,
Paris, France.
Architect:
Henri Sauvage,
1873–1932.

Detail, front door,
artist Maurice Neumont's
house, 1900s.
Place Calvert 1,
Paris, France.
Architect:
Louis Brachet,
1877–1968.

Above:
Paul Hankar, architect, 1859–1901.
Artist: Adolphe Crespin, 1859–1944.

Belgium

Right:
Façade,
Hotel Ciamberlani, 1897,
Defaqzstraat 48,
Brussels, Belgium.
Architect:
Paul Hankar.

REPUBLICA ARGENTINA
EMBAJADA

This page and opposite:
Front doors, 1900– 02,
Rue Vanderschrick,
Saint Gilles,
Brussels, Belgium.
Architect:
Ernest Blérot,
1870–1957, Belgium.

Stained glass window,
1902,
Rue Vilain XIIII 9–11,
Brussels, Belgium.
Architect:
Ernest Blérot.

Ern. Blerot

Decorative sgraffito panels above front doors, 1900–02, Rue Vanderschrick, Saint Gilles, Brussels, Belgium. Architect: Ernest Blérot.

Sgraffito decoration,
Chaussée de Waterloo 22,
1900–02,
Saint Gilles,
Brussels, Belgium.
Architect:
Ernest Blérot,
1870–1957, Belgium.

Sgraffito decoration,
Rue Vanderschrick 7,
1900–02,
Saint Gilles,
Brussels, Belgium.
Architect:
Ernest Blérot.

Right and opposite:
Decorative sgraffito panels above front doors, Brussels, Belgium.

Right and opposite:
Glazed tiles, 1900s, Avenue de Tervueren, Woluwe-Saint-Pierre, Brussels, Belgium.

Maison De Beck, 1893,
Avenue Paul Dejaer 9,
Saint Gilles,
Brussels, Belgium.
Architect:
Gustave Strauven,
1878–1919.

Façade,
Maison St Cyr, 1903,
apartment building,
Square Ambiorix 11,
Brussels, Belgium.
Architect:
Gustave Strauven.

Left:
Detail, leaded glass window,
Marjolaine, 1904,
Antiques shop,
Rue de la Madeleine 7,
Brussels, Belgium.
Architect:
Léon Sneyers
1877–1948.

Opposite:
Façade, 1902,
Lutherstraat 28,
Brussels, Belgium.
Architect:
Gustave Strauven.

Above:
Belgian postage stamp.

Right:
Front door,
Hotel Solvay, 1894,
Avenue Louise 224,
Brussels, Belgium.
Architect:
Victor Horta,
1861–1947.

Above:
House number,
Hotel Solvay, 1894,
Avenue Louise 224,
Brussels, Belgium.
Architect:
Victor Horta.

Left :
Window and façade,
Horta Museum, 1901.
Rue Americaine 25,
Brussels, Belgium.
Architect:
Victor Horta.

Left:
Detail, stained glass door,
Wallpaper,
Hotel Tassel, 1892–93,
Rue Paul-Emile Janson 6,
Brussels, Belgium.
Architect: Victor Horta.

Above:
Belgian postage stamp.

Right:
Façade,
Horta Museum, 1901,
Rue Americaine 25,
Brussels, Belgium.
Architect:
Victor Horta.

Left:
Façade,
Hotel van Eetvelde,
1898–1900,
Parmerstonian 2–4,
Brussels, Belgium.
Architect:
Victor Horta.

This page and opposite:
Brass door handles
and mail slots, 1900s.
Brussels, Belgium.

LETTRES

Lettres

Right:
Window,
Hotel Hannon, 1902.
Avenue de la Jonction 1,
Saint Gilles,
Brussels, Belgium.
Architect:
Jules Brunfaut,
1852–1942, Belgium.
Sculptor:
Victor Rousseau,
1865–1954.

H

This page:
Details,
and opposite:
Façade,
sgraffito panels,
Maison Les Hiboux, 1899,
(The Owls),
Brugmannlaan 55,
Brussels, Belgium.
Architect:
Édouard Pelseneer,
1870–1947.

Les hiboux

Above:
Belgian postage stamp.

Right and opposite:
Cauchie House,
Rue des Francs 5,
Etterbeek,
Brussels, Belgium.
Architect:
Paul Cauchie,
1875–1952.

PAR NOUS
POUR NOUS

Above:
Stained glass window,
Brussels, Belgium.

Right:
Stained glass window,
Rue Vanderschrick 19,
Brussels, Belgium.
Architect:
Ernest Blérot,
1870–1957.

Opposite:
Artist's studio,
Avenue du Lac 6,
1902,
Brussels, Belgium.
Architect:
Ernest Delune,
1859–1947.

This page:
Ceramic tiles,
La Grande Maison
de Blanc, 1896–97,
Rue du Marché aux
Poulets 32–34,
Brussels, Belgium.
Architect:
Oscar François.
Artist:
Henri Privat-Livemont.
1861–1936.

Opposite:
"Old England" building,
1899,
Musical
Instrument Museum
(formerly
department store),
Rue Montagne
de la Cour / Hofberg 2,
Brussels, Belgium.
Architect:
Paul Saintenoy,
1862–1952.
Architect, teacher,
architectural historian,
and writer.

Notable works:
Hotel Baron Lunden,
Brussels, Belgium.
Maison Losseau,
Mons, Belgium.

OLD ENGLAND

Façade,
Steiner School,
1899–1903.
Formerly
Maison du Peuple
(Socialist party).
Volksstraat 40,
Antwerp, Belgium.
Architect:
Emiel van Averbeke,
1876–1946.

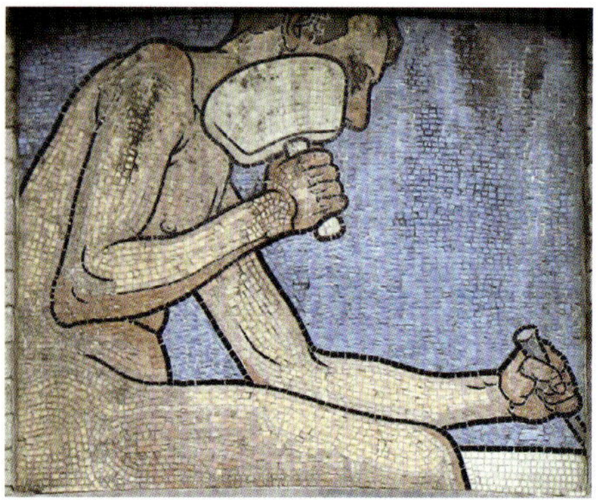

Above:
Detail,
and right:
Entrance,
and below:
Rooftop sculture,
Steiner School,
1899–1903.
Formerly
Maison du Peuple
(Socialist party).
Volksstraat 40,
Antwerp, Belgium.
Architect:
Emiel van Averbeke,
1876–1946

Opposite:
Façade, 1904,
Waterloostraat 27,
Zurenborg,
Antwerp, Belgium.
Architect:
Jacques De Weerdt,
1867–1942.

Balcony, 1909,
Waterloostraat 45,
Zurenborg,
Antwerp, Belgium.
Architect:
H. Van Steenbergen,
1864–1931.
Bow window:
Louis Hendrik.

Window, 1904,
Waterloostraat 26–28,
Zurenborg,
Antwerp, Belgium.
Architect:
Jacques de Weerdt.

Above:
Belgian postage stamp.

Left:
Het bootje,
(The little boat), 1901,
Schilderstraat 2,
Antwerp, Belgium.
Owner:
Shipbuilder P. Rouis.
Architect:
Frans-Smet Verhas,
1851–1925.

This page and opposite:
Faience panels,
Four Seasons, 1899,
Winter, Spring,
Autumn and Summer,
Generaal van Merlenstraat
27–30,
Zurenborg,
Antwerp, Belgium.
Architect:
Joseph Bascourt,
1863–1927.

This page and opposite:
Tile and sgraffito decorative panels, 1900s.
Zurenborg,
Antwerp, Belgium.

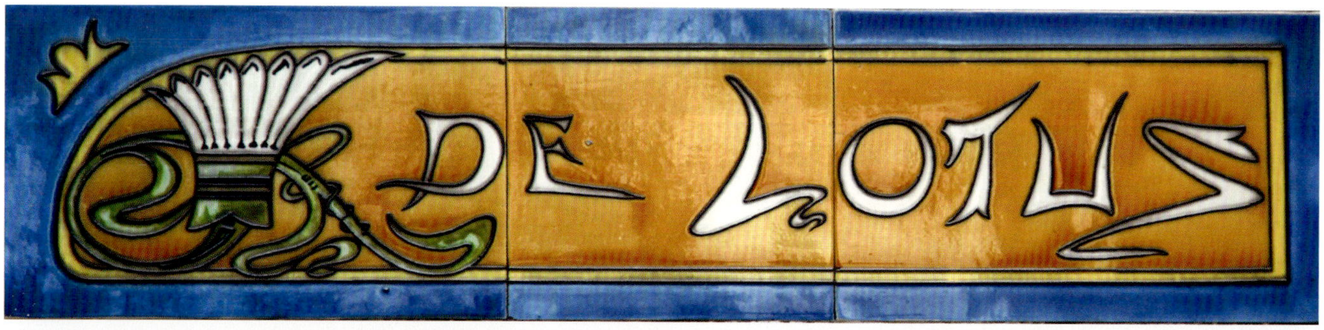

Tiles,
De Lotus, 1901,
Transvaalstraat 52–54,
Zurenborg,
Antwerp, Belgium.
Architect:
Joseph Bascourt.

Napoleon,
mosaic, 1905,
Waterloostraat 30,
Zurenborg,
Antwerp, Belgium.
Architect:
Jacques De Weerdt.

Decorative tiles, 1900s.
Waterloostraat 12,
Zurenborg,
Antwerp, Belgium.
Architect:
August Cols and
Alfred Defever.

Above and right:
Bluebell window and panel decoration, 1899, Generaal van Merlenstraat 99, Zurenborg, Antwerp, Belgium. Architect: Joseph Bascourt.

Center:
De Pauw, (The Peacock), 1897, Waterloostraat 8, Zurenborg, Antwerp, Belgium. Artist: August Cols, 1870–1947.

Right:
Detail, mosaic, 1898, Cogels-Osylei 44, Zurenborg, Antwerp, Belgium. Architect: T. Van den Bossche.

Opposite:
Façade, Les Mouettes, 1897–1905, Waterloostraat 39, Zurenborg, Antwerp, Belgium. Architect: Jacques De Weerdt,

MOUETT

Maison Den Tijd, Den Dag and De Nacht, (The Time, The Day, The Night), 1903, Waterloostraat 59–61, Zurenborg, Antwerp, Belgium.
Architects:
August Cols, 1870–1947,
and
Alfred Defever, 1874–1924.

Notable works:
Maison ou Villa De Waterlelies, Cogels-Osylei 42, 1900,
Ensemble De Pauw, Waterloostraat 8–12, 1900.
Ensemble Notus, Zephyr, Eurus en Boreas, Grotehondstraat 38–40, 46–48, 1901,
Ensemble Den Tijd, Waterloostraat 55 à 63, 1903.
Plantin en Moretuslei 110–116, 1906.
Lange Lozanastraat 43, 1906.
Maison De Zonnewijzer, Cogels-Osylei 59, 1909.
Ensemble Het Water, Generaal Capiaumontstraat 22 et Velodroomstraat 13, 1911.

TIJD
59
61

Façade, 1904,
Cogels-Osylei 80,
Zurenborg,
Antwerp, Belgium.
Architect:
Jacques De Weerdt.

Left:
Bee mosaic, 1908,
Oostenstraat 30,
Zurenborg,
Antwerp, Belgium.
Architect:
Jacques De Weerdt.

Right:
Balcony, 1904,
Waterloostraat 53,
Zurenborg,
Antwerp, Belgium.
Architect:
Adolphe Van Coppernolle,
1881–1953.

Far right:
Window, 1907,
Oostenstraat 34,
Zurenborg,
Antwerp, Belgium.
Architect:
Jacques De Weerdt.

Right:
Metal balcony, 1912,
Generaal
van Merlenstraat 39,
Zurenborg,
Antwerp, Belgium.
Ernest Stordiau,
1855–1937.

Left:
Wrought iron balcony, Waterloostraat 63, Zurenborg, Antwerp, Belgium. Architect: August Cols and Alfred Defever, 1874–1929.

Right:
Façade, 1906,
Transvaalstraat 30,
Zurenborg,
Antwerp, Belgium.
Architect:
Jacques De Weerdt.

Façade, house, 1901–02,
Beeldhouwersstraat 22,
(Street of Sculptors),
Zurenborg,
Antwerp, Belgium.
Architect:
Guillaume van Oenen,
1850–1899.

Right:
Entrance door,
Waterloostraat 28,
Zurenborg,
Antwerp, Belgium.
Architect:
Jacques De Weerdt.

Far right:
Entrance door,
Waterloostraat 10,
Zurenborg,
Antwerp, Belgium.

Right:
Entrance door, 1901,
Schilderstraat 2,
Antwerp, Belgium.
Architect:
Frans Smet-Werhas,
1851–1925.

Far right:
Entrance door, 1901,
Plaatsnijdersstraat 1,
Antwerp, Belgium.
Architect:
Frans Smet-Werhas.

Above:
Tiles, Boreas House, 1898,
Transvaalstraat 56,
Zurenborg,
Antwerp, Belgium.
Architect:
Joseph Bascourt,
1863–1927.

Left:
Iris de Lischbloem mosaic,
(Calla lillies), and
wrought iron canopy
and banister,
front door, 1898,
Cogels-Osylei 44,
Zurenborg,
Antwerp, Belgium.
Architect:
T. Van den Bossche.

Tiled clock façade, 1904.
Court of Love and
Precaution Alms House,
Voorschoterlaan 79,
Rotterdam,
The Netherlands.
Architect:
Gerrit Spelt.
Tiles:
Rozenburg.

The Netherlands

EN VOORZORG
ROZENBURG

This page and opposite:
Tiles and façade, 1901.
Schiedamsingel 161–165,
Rotterdam,
The Netherlands.
Architects:
D. van Ameijden van Duijm & Zn,
1814–1890.

This page and opposite:
Details and façade, decorative tiled building, 1902.
Laan Van Meerdervoort 164, The Hague, The Netherlands.
Architect: J. Olthuis, 1851–1921.

Ornate wood and metal front door, 1896, Smidswater 26, The Hague, The Netherlands. Architects: Johannes Petrus, 1849-n/a, Josephus Lorrie, 1861–1944.

Left:
Detail,
brass door handle,
and below:
Mail slot,
Smidswater 26,
The Hague,
The Netherlands.
Architect:
Johannes Petrus
Josephus Lorrie,
1861–1944.

Right:
Detail,
Kettingstraat 25,
The Hague,
The Netherlands.

Far right:
Façade, 1901–02,
Veenkade 33,
The Hague,
The Netherlands.
Architect:
W.B. van Liefland,
1857–1919.

Other works:
Scheveningen Pier.
Wandelhoofd
Koningin Wilhelmina,
Scheveningen.
Palace Hotel, Scheveningen.

Opposite:
Villa De Zeemeeuw,
(The Seagull), 1901–04,
Wagenaarweg 30,
Scheveningen,
The Hague,
The Netherlands.
Architect:
Henry Clemens
van de Velde,
1863–1957.
Painter, architect,
interior designer,
and art theorist.

Other works:
Haus Hohe Pappeln,
Weimar, Germany.
Haus Schulenburg,
Gera, Germany.
Villa Esche,
Chemnitz, Germany.

Right:
Decorative tiles,
clothing store,
Noordeinde 4–6,
The Hague,
The Netherlands.

Center:
Tiles,
Zoutmanstraat 2,
The Hague,
The Netherlands.

Below:
Glazed tiles, 1900s.
Hoogstraat 9,
The Hague,
The Netherlands.

Above:
Delft tiles, doorway,
Slaapkamer Ameublementen,
(Bedroom furniture),
Zoutmanstraat 18,
The Hague,
The Netherlands.

Left:
Entrance panel glazed tiles,
S. Van Leeuwen
antiques store, 1900s.
Noordeinde 164,
The Hague,
The Netherland.
Tiles:
Plateelbakkerij.

Tiled signage,
Apotheek
(Pharmacy), 1900s,
Kanaalweg 53,
The Hague,
The Netherlands.

Right and opposite:
Tiled entry panels, 1900s.
The Hague,
The Netherlands.

Right:
Detail,
decorative tiles,
1880,
Pietheinstraat 89,
The Hague,
The Netherlands.

Right:
Voetboogsteeg 3,
Centrum, Amsterdam,
M. Buttinghausen
Photografie Artistique,
1900.
Centrum, Amsterdam,
The Netherlands.
Architect:
Gerrit A. van Arkel,
1858–1918.

Other work:
Villa Betty, Amsterdam.

Left and below:
Details, decorations,
M. Buttinghausen
Photografie Artistique,
1895–1900,
Helios Building,
Spui 15,
Centrum, Amsterdam,
The Netherlands.
Architect:
Gerrit A. van Arkel.

Cafe, former clothing store, 1901–1902, Utrechtsestraat 19, Amsterdam, The Netherlands. Architects: J. A. Schmitz, A. Jacob & Willem Oldeweldt, 1865–1906.

House number, Amsterdam, The Netherlands.

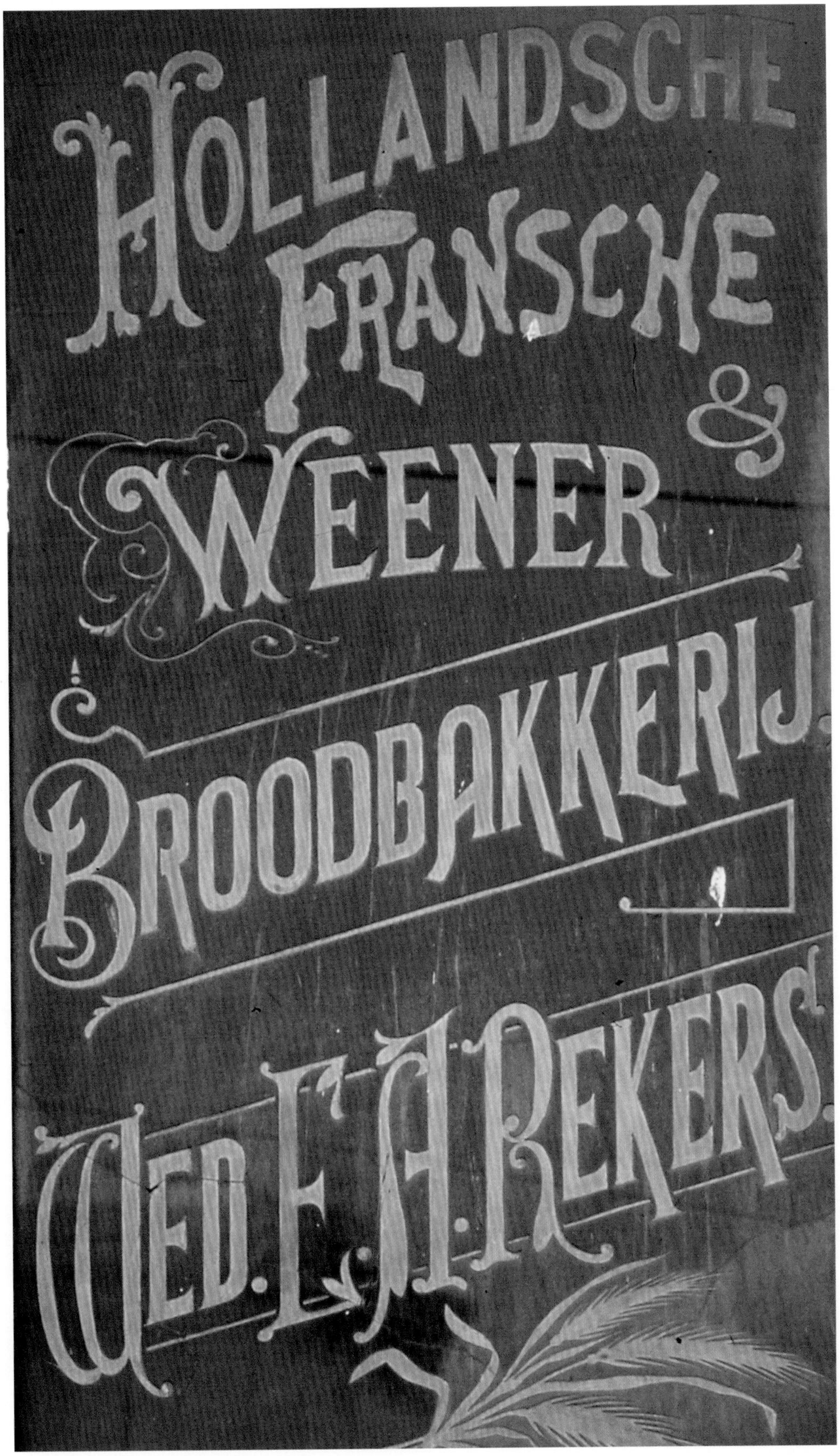

Sign board, 1890–1910,
Prinsengracht
at Leidsestraat,
Amsterdam,
The Netherlands.

CAFE
TAUR

CAFE

Opposite:
Details,
The American Hotel, 1902,
Leidsekade 97,
Amsterdam,
The Netherlands.
Architect:
Willem Krumhout,
1864–1940.

Left:
Tiled façade,
Haarlemmerstraat 60,
Amsterdam,
The Netherlands.

Above:
Detail, and right:
Façade detail,
Cinema /Restaurant,
Pathe Buitenhof, 1904,
Buitenhof 22,
The Hague,
The Netherlands.
Architect:
Johan Mutters,
1858–1930.

Other works:
Savoy Hotel, Scheveningen,
Eisenhowerlaan 132,
The Hague.

Above and right:
Façade, 1903,
Laan van
Meerdervoort 215,
The Hague,
The Netherlands.
Architect:
L.A.H. de Wolf,
1871–1923.

Above:
The author's first photograph taken of the Liberty style, 1969.
Grandi Magazzini Duilio, 1927–1930,
48 Lungomare de Viareggio, Viareggio, Toscana, Italy.
Architect:
Alfredo Belluomini, 1892–1964.

Italy

Right:
Casa Jung Calabrese (ex Mordo),
1901–04,
Via Giosue Carducci 11, Trieste, Italy
Architect:
Giovanni Maria Mosco, 1861–1924.

Right:
Apartment building,
1900s,
Via di Romagna 24,
Trieste.

Opposite:
Gilded façade,
Casa Righetti,1903,
Via Galileo 24
Trieste, Italy.
Architect:
Giusto Righetti.

Above:
Mosaic date,
and right:
door, 1907,
Via Commerciale 23,
Trieste, Italy.
Architect:
Giorgio Zaninovich,
1876–1946.

Gilded façade,
Casa Righetti, 1903,
Via Galileo 24.
Trieste, Italy.
Architect:
Giusto Righetti.

Mosaic dragon and chimney pots, roof, Casa Battló, 1904–06. Barcelona, Spain. Architect: Antoni Gaudi, 1852–1926.

Spain

"The straight line belongs to man, the curved line belongs to God." Antoni Gaudi.

16

Left:
Interior,
Basilica de la
Sagrada Familia, 1882–,
Barcelona, Spain.
Architect:
Antoni Gaudi.

Right:
Balconies,
Casa Battló, 1905–07,
Casa dels ossos,
(House of Bones),
Passeig de Gracia 43,
Barcelona, Spain.
Architect:
Antoni Gaudi.

Above:
Postage stamp, Spain.

Left:
Casa Battló, 1905–07,
Casa dels ossos,
(House of Bones),
Passeig de Gracia 43,
Barcelona, Spain.
Architect:
Antoni Gaudi.

Above:
Detail, mosaic,
and right:
Casa Battló, 1905–07,
Casa dels ossos,
(House of Bones),
Passeig de Gracia 43,
Barcelona, Spain.
Architect:
Antoni Gaudi.

Right:
Detail, rear façade,
Casa Comalat,
1909–11,
Carrer de Corsega 316,
Barcelona, Spain.
Architect:
Salvador Valeri i Pupurull.

Left:
Mosaic bench,
Guell Park, 1914,
Barcelona, Spain.
Architect:
Antoni Gaudi.

Left:
Mosaic signage,
Guell Park, 1914,
Barcelona, Spain.
Architect:
Antoni Gaudi.

Right:
Mosaic lizard, Guell Park, 1914, Barcelona, Spain. Architect: Antoni Gaudi.

Above:
Ceramic tiles,
Casa Jaume Forn, 1904–09,
Carrer de Roger de Lluria 82,
Barcelona, Spain.
Architect:
Jeroni F. Granell i Manresa.

Left:
Stained glass bay window,
Casa Cama i Escurra, 1902,
Carrer Gran de Gràcia 15,
Barcelona, Spain.
Architect:
Francesc Berenguer
i Mestres, 1866–1914.

Right:
Mosaic detail,
and below and opposite:
Palau de la musica
Catalana, (Music Palace),
1905–08,
Barcelona, Spain.
Architect:
Lluis Domenech i Montaner,
1850–1923.

Other works:
Casa Fuster, Madrid.
Ateneu Obrer.
Canet de Mar.
Casa Gasull, Reus.
Cementerio de Comillas,
Comillas.

Right:
Inlaid mosaic wall decoration and metal balcony, Las Ramblas 84, Barcelona, Spain.

Right:
Mosaic decoration, apartment building, Barcelona, Spain.

Opposite:
Façade, apartment building, 1903, Carrer de Bailèn 113, Barcelona, Spain.
Architect:
Antoni Gallissà i Soqué, 1861–1903.

PERLAS
La Metalurgia R. Ibáñez
BERLIN 95
SDAD LDA
TEL. 4300916
BARCELONA

PURÉS
BERLIN 95
SDAD LDA

F.ca de PASTAS ALIMENTICIAS
TAPIOCAS
Bombons

Right:
Wood and metal door,
1900s.
Barcelona, Spain.

Far right:
Wall decoration,
El Indio
clothing store, 1922,
(now a restaurant)
Carrer del Carme 24,
El Raval,
Barcelona, Spain.
Architect:
Vilaro i Valls.

FARMACIA NADAL
ANTIGA Dr. MASÓ ARUMÍ
12

312

FUNDADA en 1562
FARMACIA
NUK
HOMEOPATIA
EN ESTA FARMACIA
RAPID CONTROL
BLITZ
LIPOSOMIAL
Plantas Medicinales
RELAXUL
relajante natural

Glass signage,
M. Boué,
Las Ramblas 31,
Barcelona, Spain.

Tiled signage,
Casellas Farmacia,
pharmacy,
Carrer del Carme 84,
Barcelona, Spain.
Mosaics:
Lluís Brú Salelles,
1868–1952.

Façade,
El Indio
clothing store, 1922,
(now a restaurant)
Carrer del Carme 24,
El Raval,
Barcelona, Spain.
Decorator:
Vilaro i Valls.

Shop signage,
S. Ferri Jewelers,
Barcelona, Spain.

Signage,
Casa Labra Restaurant,
Calle Tetuán 12,
Madrid, Spain.

Right:
Metal grille window, 1890s, Cadiz, Spain.

Opposite:
Forn des Teatre, 1916, now a restaurant, Plaça de Weyler 9, Palma de Mallorca, Spain.

HORNO
Forn des Teatre
JAUME ALEMANY
9

Above:
Bronze lion's head,
Postbox, 1896.
Bilbao, Spain.

Right:
Estación de Santander,
"La Concordia"
(Santander Station),
1898–1902,
Calle Bailen 2,
Bilbao, Spain.
Architect:
Severino Achúcarro,
1841–1910,
Engineer:
Valentín Gorbeña.

TANDER A BILBAO

Elevador do Carmo,
1900–02,
Santa Justa Elevator,
Lisbon, Portugal.
Engineer:
Raoul Mesnier du Ponsard,
1848–1914.

Other works:
Ascensor da Gloria,
Lisbon.
Ascensor da Bica,
Lisbon.

Portugal

Metal and
stained glass decoration,
Joalharia Ferreira Marques,
1926,
Praça Dom Pedro IV 7–9,
Lisbon, Portugal.

Above:
Austrian postage stamp.

Austria

Right:
Karlsplatz
Stadtbahn Station, 1899,
Vienna, Austria,
Architect:
Otto Koloman Wagner,
1841–1918.

ARLSPLATZ
CAFE
Kaffee Meinl
Meinl Kaffee Meinl

Above:
Detail,
and right:
Clock,
Karlsplatz
Stadtbahn Station, 1899,
Karlsplatz,
Vienna, Austria,
Architect:
Otto Koloman Wagner.

Right:
Ceramic vase,
Promenade,
Stadtpark,
Vienna, Austria.

Above:
Austrian postage stamp, "Judith and the Head of Holofernes", 1901. Artist: Gustav Klimt, 1862–1918.

Left:
Façade detail, Secession Building, 1897, Friedrichstrasse 12, Vienna, Austria. Architect: Joseph Maria Olbrich. Designers: Koloman Moser, and Gustav Klimt. Joseph Maria Olbrich, 1874–1951.

Left:
Mosaic bowl, Secession Building, 1897, Friedrichstrasse 12, Vienna, Austria. Architect: Joseph Maria Olbrich. Designers: Koloman Moser and Gustav Klimt. Joseph Maria Olbrich.

Right:
Marble and mosaic decoration,
Zum weissen Engel (White Angel) pharmacy,
1901–02,
Bognerstrasse 9,
Vienna, Austria.
Architect:
Oskar Laske,
1874–1951.

Opposite:
Gold ornament façade,
Medallion House,
1898–99,
Linke Wienzeile 38,
Vienna, Austria.
Architect:
Otto Koloman Wagner.
Decoration:
Koloman Moser.

Above:
Koloman Moser
self-portrait, 1903.

Right:
Detail, mosaic mural,
"The Five Continents",
1894–96,
Kärntner Strasse 16,
Vienna, Austria.
Artist:
Eduard Veith,
1858–1925.

Right:
Detail, iron bridge,
Hohe Brücke, 1904,
Tiefer Graben 2,
Vienna, Austria
Architect:
Josef Hackhofer,
1863–1917.

Opposite:
Ceramic tiles,
Majolikahaus, 1898–99,
Linke Wienzeile 40,
Vienna, Austria,
Architect:
Otto Kolomon Wagner.

Slovenia

Right:
Detail, façade, formerly Palace kmeke posojilnice, Agricultural Bank Building, 1900s, Trdinova ulica 8, Ljubljana, Slovenia.

Right:
Metal window grille decoration, Tavarjeva ulica 6, Ljubljana, Slovenia.

Tower,
Čudnova hiša, 1901,
Cigaletova ulica 6,
Ljubljana, Slovenia.
Architect:
Ciril Metod Koch,
1867–1925.

Above:
Candelabra,
The Cobblers' Bridge,
1931,
Ljubljana, Slovenia.
Architect:
Joze Plecnik.

Right:
Pircova hisa, 1905–06,
Cigaletova ulica 5,
Lubljana, Slovenia.
Architect:
Ciril Metod Kosch.

Left:
Hauptmann House,
Originally built in 1873,
remodeled in 1904 in
Vienna Secession style,
Wolfova ulica 2,
Ljubljana, Slovenia.
Architect:
Jože Plecnik,
1872–1957.
Following the earthquake
of 1895, remodeled by
Ciril Metod Koch.

Czech Republic

Above:
Czech Republic
postage stamp.

Right:
Façade,
U Obecni dum,
(Municipal House),
1905–11,
Namesti Republiky 5,
Staré Mesto, Prague,
Czech Republic.
Architects:
Antonín Balšánek,
1865–1921 and
Osvald Polívka,
1859–1931.
Mosaic:
Zemska Bawk.

Left:
Stained glass screen, entrance, U Obecni dum, (Municipal House), 1905–11, Namesti Republiky 5, Staré Mesto, Prague, Czech Republic. Artist: Alphonse Mucha.

Interior artists and sculptors include Jan Preisler, Ladislav Šaloun and Alphonse Mucha.

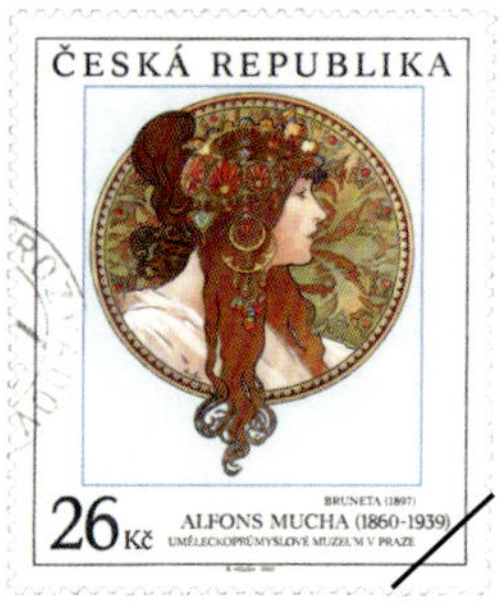

Above:
Czech Republic
postage stamp.
This page:
Mural,
and opposite:
Clock,
The French Restaurant,
U Obecni dum,
(Municipal House),
1905–11,
Namesti Republiky 5,
Staré Mesto, Prague,
Czech Republic.
Architects:
Antonín Balšánek and
Osvald Polívka.
Interior artists and
sculptors include
Jan Preisler,
Ladislav Šaloun and
Alphonse Mucha.

:LÉKÁRNA:

Above:
Majolica panel, 1910.
Women and Carp,
Kaprova Street,
Staré Mesto, Prague,
Czech Republic.
Sculptor: Richard Luksck,
1872–1936.

Right:
Door with clock,
1072 Staré Mesto, Prague,
Czech Republic.

Opposite:
Dum U Dorfleru, 1905,
Hlavni Mesto,
Prague, Czech Republic.
Architect: Jiri Just.

U DORFLERŮ
POSTAVENO
L.P. 1905

"1900",
sgraffito pediment,
Prague, Czech Republic.

Right:
Entrance door grille,
and opposite:
Trade and Industry
mosaic, 1901–04,
U Nováku (Novaks)
department store,
Vodickova 30,
Prague, Czech Republic.
Architect:
Osvald Polka,
1859–1931.
Artist:
Jan Preisler,
1872–1918.

This page and opposite:
Mosaics,
Zemska Bank building,
1909-11,
Na Prikope Street,
Prague, Czech Republic.
Architect:
Osvald Poilka.
Artist:
Jan Preisler.

HOTEL

Left and opposite:
Detail,
Grand Hotel Europa,
1903–05,
Wenceslas Square,
Prague, Czech Republic.
Architects:
Bedrich Bendelmayer,
1871–1932
and Alois Dryák,
1872–1932.

Poland

Left:
Leaded glass transom,
Redolfi Restaurant,
Rynek Glowny 38,
Krakow, Poland.

Above:
Hungarian postage stamp.

Hungary

Right:
Gellért Thermal Baths, 1911–18, Kelenhegy út 4, Budapest, Hungary. Architects: Izidor Sterk, 1860–1935, Armin Hegedüs, 1869–1945, and Artur Sebestyen, 1868–1945.

Opposite:
Gellért Thermal Baths, 1911–18, Kelenhegy út 4, Budapest, Hungary. Architects: Izidor Sterk, Armin Hegedüs, and Artur Sebestyen.

Above:
"Cinderella" stamp, 1912,
Horticultural Expo,
Budapest, Hungary.

Right:
Our Lady of Hungary,
Torok Bank House, 1906.
Szervita tér,
Budapest, Hungary.
Architects:
Henrik Böhm and
Armin Hegedüs,
1869–1945.
Mosaic:
Miksa Roth,
1865–1944.

This page and opposite:
Mosaic and Majolica,
Sepulchral vault of
Sandor Schmidl, 1903,
Jewish Cemetery,
Kozma u. 6,
Budapest, Hungary.
Designed by
Bela Lajta,
1873–1920
and
Odon Lechner,
1845–1914.

Detail,
Façade,
Formerly Árkád Bazár,
(Arcade Bazaar), 1909,
Toy Store,
Dohány u. 22–24,
Belvaros,
Budapest, Hungary.
Architects:
Vago Brothers.
Ceramics:
Zsolnay.

Above:
Detail,
Façade,
Formerly Árkád Bazár,
(Arcade Bazaar), 1909,
Toy Store,
Dohány u. 22–24,
Belvaros,
Budapest, Hungary.
Architects:
Vago Brothers.
Ceramics:
Zsolnay.

Russian Federation

Interior detail,
The Moscow Choral
Synagogue, 1906,
Bol'shoy
Spasoglinishchevskiy
Pereulok 10,
Moscow,
Russian Federation.
Architect:
Roman Klein,
1858–1924.

Tiled mural,
Metropol Hotel,
1899–1905.
Teatral'nyy Proyezd 2,
Moscow,
Russian Federation.
Architects:
William Walcott,
1874–1943,
Lev Kekuschev,
Vladimir Shuckhov.
Artists:
Mikhail Vrubel,
Alexander Golovin,
Nikolai Andreev.

Above:
Detail, tiles,
Metropol Hotel,
1899–1905.
Teatral'nyy Proyezd 2,
Moscow,
Russian Federation.

Tiled mural,
Metropol Hotel, 1905,
2 Teatralniy Proezd,
Moscow,
Russian Federation.
Architect:
William Walcott.

Façade, 1990s,
Mesrutiyet Caddesi 23,
Galata,
Istanbul, Turkey.

Far left:
Entrance,
Casa Botter, 1900–1901,
Istiklal Caddesi 235,
Beyoglu,
Istanbul, Turkey.
Architect:
Raimondo D'Aronco,
1857–1932.

Left:
Detail, "Bees" metal gate,
8 Ravouna Apartments,
1901–06,
Istiklal Caddesi 201,
Beyoglu, Istanbul, Turkey.
Architects:
Konstantinos P. Kyriakidis,
1881–1942
and
Aleksandros D. Neokosmos.

Above:
Window grille,
Beyoglu,
Istanbul, Turkey.

Left:
Former office building,
now Pera Parma Hotel,
MeQrutiyet Caddesi 7,
Beyoglu,
Istanbul, Turkey.

Cafe Markiz, 1920s.
Istiklal Caddesi 360–362,
Beyoglu,
Istanbul, Turkey.
Architect:
Alexandre Vallaury, 1850
1921.
Ceramic tiles, 1905.
Artist: J.A. Arnoux,
1877–1960.
Produced in France by
Ch. Boulanger
at Choisy-Le-Roi.
Note: All panels were
shipped from France,
only "Spring" and
"Autumn" arrived intact.

LE PRINTEMPS

Terracotta,
Michelin House, 1911,
Michelin Tyre
Company Ltd.,
81 Fulham Road,
Chelsea, London, UK.
Architect:
François Espinasse,
1880–1925.
Tile design:
Gilardoni & Cie.

United Kingdom

81

Michelin monogram,
metal grille,
Michelin House, 1911,
Michelin Tyre
Company Ltd.,
81 Fulham Road,
Chelsea, London, UK.
Architect:
François Espinasse.

Detail, metal monogram,
Michelin House, 1911.
Michelin Tyre
Company Ltd.,
81 Fulham Road,
Chelsea, London, UK.
Architect:
François Espinasse.

Detail, ceramic tiles,
Michelin House, 1911,
Michelin Tyre
Company Ltd.,
81 Fulham Road,
Chelsea, London, UK.
Architect:
François Espinasse.

Right and below:
Decorative tiles,
Michelin House, 1911,
Michelin Tyre
Company Ltd.,
81 Fulham Road,
Chelsea, London, UK.
Pictorial panels design:
Gilardoni Fils, Paris.

In 1940, because of the risk of bombing during the Second World War, Michelin removed the three stained glass windows. They were carefully packed into wooden crates and sent to the Stoke-on-Trent factory for safe keeping. After the war, Michelin returned its headquarters to London and planned to reinstall the windows. However, they could not be found.
After a long search, suppliers were found, and replicas of the windows and cupolas were made using original drawings, photos and posters.

Left:
"Bibendum",
stained glass window,
Michelin House, 1911,
Michelin Tyre
Company Ltd.,
81 Fulham Road,
Chelsea, London, UK.
Architect:
François Espinasse.

This page and opposite:
"Bibendum",
stained glass windows,
Michelin House, 1911,
Michelin Tyre
Company Ltd.,
81 Fulham Road,
Chelsea, London, UK.
Architect:
François Espinasse:

Right:
Lithograph poster,
Le Coup de la Semelle
Michelin,
(The Middle Sole), 1905.
Artist: Marius Rossillon
(known as O'Galop),
1867–1946.

Left:
Advertising poster,
Michelin Pneu Velo.
Artist: Marius Rossillon
(known as O'Galop)

Note:
The Michelin Man character
was created by O'Galop
in 1898.

Right:
"Queen of Time" clock
c. 1925,
Selfridges Department Store,
400 Oxford Street, W1,
London.
Sculptor:
Gilbert William Bayes RA,
1872–1953.

Left:
Britain and the Orient,
Bronze door caryatids,
P&O Building, 1906–07,
14–16 Cockspur Street,
London, UK.
Architect:
Arthur T. Bolton,
1864–1945.
Sculptor:
W.B. Fagan,
1860–1948.

Above and right:
Stained glass windows,
The Queens Public House,
1898–1901.
Tottenham Lane,
Crouch End,
London, UK.
Architect:
John C. Hill,
1898–1901.
Stained glass design:
Cakebread Robey.

Doulton terracotta signage,
St. Pancras Public Baths
and Public Hall,
1898–1900,
Prince of Wales Road,
Camden Town,
London, UK.
Architect:
Thomas W. Aldwinckle,
1845–1920.

CRAS

HS

HALL

Above:
Glazed ceramic tile,
Booking Hall,
and right and opposite:
Metal ventilation grilles,
London Transport
Underground Station, 1907,
Edgware Road,
London, UK.
Architects:
Harry W. Ford,
1875–1947,
and
Leslie Green,
1875–1908.

Metal ventilation grille,
Mornington Crescent
London Transport
Underground Station, 1907,
Camden Town,
London, UK.
Architect:
Leslie Green.

Right:
Ticket window,
Edgware Road,
London Transport
Underground Station,
1907.
London, UK.
Architect:
Leslie Green,
1875–1908.

Far right:
Ceramic tiles,
Way out sign,
Covent Garden
London Transport
Underground Station,
1906.
London, UK.
Tiles:
H&E Smith.

Right:
Mosaic roundel,
Maida Vale
London Transport
Underground Station,
1914–15,
London, UK.
Architect:
Stanley Heaps,
1880–1962.

Left: Mosaic signage, Lexington Avenue subway station, 1918, New York, New York, USA.

United States

Left: Astor Place Subway station, 1904, New York, New York, USA.

Astor Place station is decorated with large ceramic beaver emblems, representing the beaver pelts that helped make John Jacob Astor wealthy.

La Princesse du pays de la porcelaine (The Princess from the Land of Porcelain), and below: Harmony in Blue and Gold, The Peacock Room, 1876–77. Detail, wall decoration, oil paint and gold leaf on canvas, Freer Gallery of Art, Washington, DC , USA. Artist: James Abbott McNeil Whistler, 1834–1903.

Left:
Leaded glass window,
Shearith Israel Synagogue, 1897,
270th Street and
Central Park West,
New York, NY, USA.
Designer:
Louis Comfort Tiffany,
1848–1933.

Above:
Terracotta pillar, 1911,
Formerly J.L. Kesner
dry goods emporium,
Sixth Avenue
and 23rd Street,
New York, NY, USA.
Architects:
Taylor and Levy.
Hartford Faience Tiles.

Left:
U.S. postage stamp.

Observer Hotel, 1909,
George Street 69,
The Rocks, Sydney,
NSW, Australia,
Architects:
Halligan & Wilton.

Australia

Stained glass window,
1890s,
private residence,
Perth, W. Australia.

Leaded glass windows,
Public House,
Melbourne, Australia.

New Zealand

Ivory Clock Tower,
The Old Arts Building,
Auckland University,
1923–26.
Auckland, New Zealand.
Architect:
Roy Alstan Lippincott,
1885–1969.

Far left top:
Bronze capital, Palacio Salvo 1919, Avenida 18 de Julio, Plaza Independencia, Montevideo, Uruguay.

Far left below:
Tiled wall decoration, Guadalajara, Mexico.

Left:
One of several figures, each representing a different musical instrument, supporting the bandstand, 1910, Plaza de Armas, Guadalajara, Mexico. Built by foundry D'art Du Val D'Osne, Paris

Uruguay & Mexico

Right:
Stained-glass ceiling,
and opposite:
Interior, elevator cage,
Gran Hotel
Ciudad de Mexico,
1899.
(formerly the
Mercantile Center)
The Zocalo,
Mexico City, Mexico.
Ceiling design:
Jacques Gruber,
1870–1936.

Right:
El Palacio de Hierro
(The Iron Palace)
department store, 1920,
Av. 20 de Noviembre 25,
Mexico City, Mexico.
Architect:
Paul Dubois,
1874–1953.
Stained glass design:
Jacques Gruber.